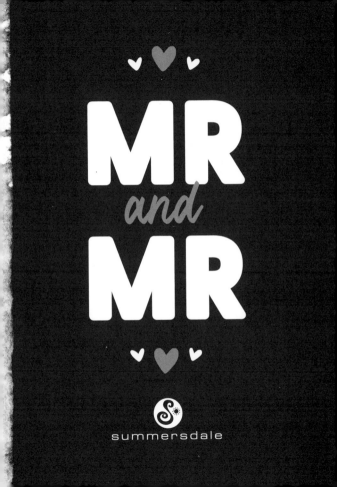

MR
and
MR

summersdale

MR AND MR

An Hachette UK Company
www.hachette.co.uk

Summersdale Publishers Ltd
Part of Octopus Publishing Group Limited
Carmelite House
50 Victoria Embankment
LONDON
EC4Y 0DZ
UK

www.summersdale.com

Printed and bound in China

ISBN: 978-1-80007-173-5

Substantial discounts on bulk quantities of Summersdale books are available to corporations, professional associations and other organizations. For details contact general enquiries: telephone: +44 (0) 1243 771107 or email: enquiries@summersdale.com.

To.....................................

From.................................

We were together – all else has long been forgotten by me.

WALT WHITMAN

LOVE

is awesome
and endless.

NEIL PATRICK HARRIS

THERE'S ONE WORD THAT UNITES ALL OF US: LOVE

We deserve to experience love fully, equally, without shame and without compromise.

ELLIOT PAGE

I CAME OUT BECAUSE
I FELL IN LOVE...
I WAS IN LOVE
WITH SOMEBODY,
AND I WANTED TO
SCREAM IT FROM
the rooftops.

GILBERT BAKER

Love will find
a way through
paths where
wolves fear
to prey.

LORD BYRON

If it's love,
it's love...
That's all
that matters.

KYLIE MINOGUE

Who, being loved, is poor?

OSCAR WILDE

NOTHING MAKES ME HAPPIER THAN YOUR LOVE

Love takes off the masks that we fear we cannot live without and know we cannot live within.

JAMES BALDWIN

I would rather look at you than all the portraits in the

WORLD.

FRANK O'HARA

We all want to love
and be loved.

MADONNA

I FALL IN LOVE
WITH YOU ALL
OVER AGAIN
EVERY TIME
I SEE YOU

I WAS AFRAID TO
SAY — I WANT TO BE
WITH YOU — SEE, HERE
I'M SHYING, BECAUSE
I REALLY WANT TO SAY,
I love you.

JOHN TASKER TO COLIN SPENCER

I cannot think of anything else all day and most of the night, but you.

COLIN SPENCER TO JOHN TASKER

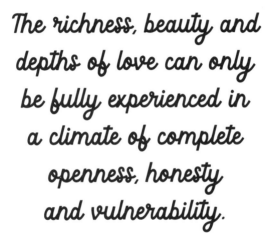

The richness, beauty and depths of love can only be fully experienced in a climate of complete openness, honesty and vulnerability.

ANTHONY VENN-BROWN

But my darling
I have that sweet
certainty that if
we were close
enough together
nothing else
would count.

STANLEY HAGGART

Marriage is a language of love, equality and inclusion.

EVAN WOLFSON

YOU'RE MY FAVOURITE EVERYTHING

I truly
believe this,
and for me,
the basis
of art is

LOVE.

DAVID HOCKNEY

Perhaps we were friends first and lovers second. But then perhaps this is what lovers are.

ANDRÉ ACIMAN

THERE'S NOTHING MORE POWERFUL THAN OUR LOVE

I LOVE YOU TO THE
LIMITS OF SPEECH
and beyond.

T. S. ELIOT

At the touch of love, everyone becomes a poet.

PLATO

Sometimes,
life is like that.
One moment.
One person.
One conversation.
And your life is
forever enriched.

MICHAEL DILLON

IT ONLY TOOK
A HEARTBEAT TO
FALL FOR YOU

A kiss makes the heart
young again and wipes
out all the years.

RUPERT BROOKE

Life without love is no life at all.

LEONARDO DA VINCI

OUR LOVE IS TOO BEAUTIFUL TO HIDE IN A CLOSET

I love you
because the
entire universe
conspired
to help me
FIND YOU.

PAULO COELHO

I'm possessed
by love,
but isn't
everybody?

FREDDIE MERCURY

**IT'S ALWAYS WRONG
TO HATE, BUT IT'S
NEVER WRONG**
to love.

LADY GAGA

YOU MAKE ME FEEL LIKE I CAN TAKE ON THE WORLD

♥

I see by the
way you look
at me that you
know that no
one loves you
more than I do.

JEAN COCTEAU

You are my sun,
my moon and
all my stars.

E. E. CUMMINGS

I LOVE YOU FOR WHO YOU ARE, AND FOR WHO I AM WHEN I'M WITH YOU

You came and I was
longing for you. You
cooled a heart that
burned with desire.

SAPPHO

I would not wish any companion in the world but you.

WILLIAM SHAKESPEARE

I'm a big
proponent of
all love winning
and love just
BEING FAB.

JONATHAN VAN NESS

It's as if when you love someone, they become your reason.

DAVID LEVITHAN

It is love,
NOT REASON,
THAT IS STRONGER
THAN DEATH.

THOMAS MANN

YOU STARTED A REVOLUTION IN MY HEART

Love has been
our survival.

AUDRE LORDE

True love is
eternal, infinite,
and always
like itself.

HONORÉ DE BALZAC

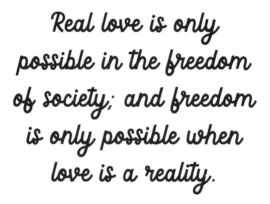

Real love is only possible in the freedom of society; and freedom is only possible when love is a reality.

EDWARD CARPENTER

The consciousness of loving and being loved brings a warmth and a richness to life that nothing else can bring.

OSCAR WILDE

WHEN I'M WITH YOU MY LIFE IS FULL OF EVERY COLOUR IN THE RAINBOW

♥

To me,

OUR LOVE

is so great that
I feel it cannot
exist without all
the world being
aware of it.

GORDON BOWSHER

MY LOVE
FOR YOU ISN'T
A CHOICE;
IT'S WHO I AM

In case you ever
foolishly forget:
I am never not
thinking of you.

VIRGINIA WOOLF

MY WHOLE DESIRE IS TO RUN UP AND DOWN THE SEA COAST

looking for you.

JOHN CAGE

It isn't possible to love and part... You can transmute love, ignore it, muddle it, but you can never pull it out of you.

E. M. FORSTER

The important
thing is not
the object of
love, but the
emotion itself.

GORE VIDAL

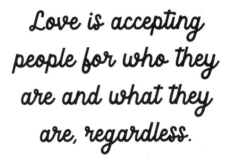

Love is accepting people for who they are and what they are, regardless.

ALICIA KEYS

I'M PROUD TO LOVE YOU

What is worth living for and what is worth dying for? The answer to each is the same. Only love.

LORD BYRON

Love does not
consist of gazing
at each other, but
in looking outward
TOGETHER
in the same
direction.

ANTOINE DE SAINT-EXUPÉRY

Love comes first.

STEPHEN FRY

TRUE LOVE IS THE FEELING THAT LINGERS AFTER EVERY KISS WE SHARE

EVERY MOMENT IS
MADE GLORIOUS
BY THE
light of love.

RUMI

If you truly
love something,
fight for it
every day.

KEIYNAN LONSDALE

I WASN'T LOOKING FOR LOVE BUT YOU FOUND ME

Love isn't something you find. Love is something that finds you.

LORETTA YOUNG

Love him and
let him love you.
Do you think anything
else under heaven
really matters?

JAMES BALDWIN

We love because it's the only true adventure.

NIKKI GIOVANNI

I CAN ALWAYS TRUST MY HEART; IT LED ME TO YOU

The brain may
take advice,
but not the

HEART,

and love, having
no geography,
knows no
boundaries.

TRUMAN CAPOTE

Love is so painful, how could you ever wish it on anybody? And love is so essential, how could you ever stand in its way?

DAVID LEVITHAN

SOME PEOPLE MEET
AND PART WAYS, OTHERS
BOND TOGETHER ON
A LIFELONG STREAM.
I GUESS YOU COULD CALL
OUR RELATIONSHIP
destiny.

ISMAIL MERCHANT

Love, the beauty of it, the joy of it and yes, even the pain of it, is the most incredible gift to give and to receive as a human being.

ELLIOT PAGE

I'm crossing my
bridges to you
my beloved –
and my eyes
are steadily on
you – my heart
is with you.

STANLEY HAGGART

YOU'RE NOT JUST
MY NUMBER
ONE; YOU'RE MY
ONE AND ONLY

*Kindness always wins...
love is best served
unconditionally.*

DAN LEVY

I already daydream
with tears of how
sweet we'll be,
meeting again.

ALLEN GINSBERG

MY HEART IS HOME WHEN I AM WITH YOU

Here are fruits, flowers, leaves and branches, and here is

MY HEART

which beats only for you.

PAUL VERLAINE

I'd never felt the feeling of love... I was completely overwhelmed by it.

TOM DALEY

THERE IS NO REMEDY
FOR LOVE BUT TO
love more.

HENRY DAVID THOREAU

OUR LOVE SHINES LIKE A RAINBOW — AND WHO DOESN'T LOVE RAINBOWS?

Love is a flame:
– we have
beaconed the
world's night.

RUPERT BROOKE

Think only of
my love and
that I am yours
always and ever.

HENRY JAMES

IN THE END, ALL THAT MATTERS IS THAT YOU ARE LOVED

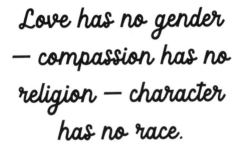

Love has no gender
— compassion has no
religion — character
has no race.

ABHIJIT NASKAR

**Seize the moments
of happiness,
love and be loved!
That is the only
reality in the world,
all else is folly.**

LEO TOLSTOY

The most powerful weapon on earth is the human

SOUL

on fire.

FERDINAND FOCH

NO ONE CAN SAY OUR LOVE IS WRONG WHEN IT FEELS SO RIGHT

Love is composed
of a single soul
inhabiting
two bodies.

ARISTOTLE

I think of you
AS IF I'M WITH YOU,
DAY OR NIGHT.

BO JUYI

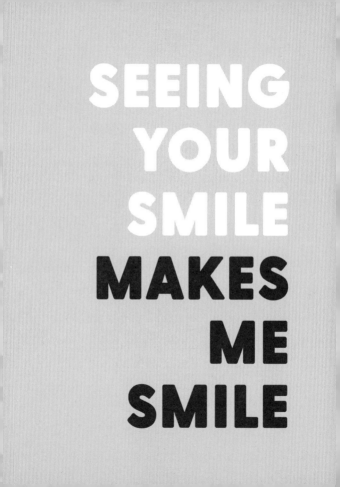

If you find
someone you
love in your life,
then hang on
to that love.

DIANA, PRINCESS OF WALES

I love you beyond expression... My love is boundless as the Sea.

DOROTHY FREEMAN

Where there is love there is life.

MAHATMA GANDHI

AFTER ALL THIS TIME EVERY KISS STILL FEELS LIKE THE FIRST

Till I loved
I never lived.

EMILY DICKINSON

LOVERS

alone wear sunlight.

E. E. CUMMINGS

EVERY DAY I FALL A LITTLE MORE IN LOVE WITH YOU

♥

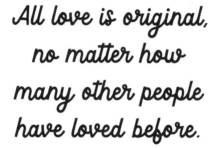

All love is original,
no matter how
many other people
have loved before.

GEORGE WEINBERG

I LOVE YOU
AND WILL LIVE AS
THOUGH YOU WERE
at my side.

RUSSELL CHENEY

If you are not
too long, I will
wait here for
you all my life.

OSCAR WILDE

Throughout my life, I have always believed in love.

RuPAUL

Love is begun
by time,
And that I see,
in passages
of proof,
Time qualifies
the spark and
fire of it.

WILLIAM SHAKESPEARE

NOTHING
COMPARES
TO MY LOVE
FOR YOU

We are saved only by love.

TENNESSEE WILLIAMS

The only
things that
matter in life
are food and

LOVE.

DAVID HOCKNEY

People should fall in love with their eyes closed. Just close your eyes. Don't look and it's magic.

ANDY WARHOL

OUT OF LOVE,

No regrets.

LANGSTON HUGHES

You can choose to love whoever you love.

JAY-Z

I WANT ALL OF MY LASTS TO BE WITH YOU

Wouldn't it be wonderful if all our letters could be published in the future in a more enlightened time. Then all the world could see how in love we are.

GORDON BOWSHER

Will you come
travel with me?
Shall we stick by
each other as
long as we live?

WALT WHITMAN

I knew that I belonged to you and you to me.

STANLEY HAGGART

I'M NEVER
ALONE BECAUSE
I NEVER STOP
THINKING OF YOU

Everybody should be allowed to be who they are, and **TO LOVE** who they love.

DOLLY PARTON

To love another
you have to
undertake some
fragment of
their destiny.

QUENTIN CRISP

LOVE IS A
human
experience,
NOT A POLITICAL
STATEMENT.

ANNE HATHAWAY

My beautiful
angel, I tell you
again that
I adore you.
I want nothing
but your
happiness.

JEAN COCTEAU

I can live
without money,
but I cannot live
without love.

JUDY GARLAND

SOMETIMES LOVE JUST HAPPENS — THAT'S WHY IT'S SO EXCITING

Love is space and
time measured
by the heart.

MARCEL PROUST

I love you as a man
can only love the
noblest and best.

HANS CHRISTIAN ANDERSEN

FALLING IN LOVE WITH YOU WAS THE BEST THING TO HAPPEN TO ME

To be fully seen by somebody, then, and be loved anyhow — this is a human offering that can border on miraculous.

ELIZABETH GILBERT

LOVE

weaves itself
from hundreds
of threads.

DAVID LEVITHAN

**EVERYTHING IS
SUDDENLY TURNED
TO GOLD!**

ALLEN GINSBERG

Without warning
as a whirlwind
swoops an oak

Love shakes
my heart.

SAPPHO

THERE'S NOTHING SWEETER THAN YOUR LOVE

♥

Follow your heart, and the things you need will come.

ELIZABETH TAYLOR

YOU TAUGHT ME HOW TO LOVE FREELY

Love in all eight
tones and all five
semitones of the
word's full octave.

STEPHEN FRY

We're all unique
and beautiful
in our own way
and entitled to
love and be loved
by whomever
we choose.

BARBRA STREISAND

Love is
friendship
set to

MUSIC.

JACKSON POLLOCK

You said we had lit [a bonfire] which shouldn't go out... We lit a fire which illumined everything and, oddly enough, was a guiding light to others.

JOHN TASKER TO COLIN SPENCER

I love you and I miss you and I want you.

COLIN SPENCER TO JOHN TASKER

YOUR LOVE CAN TURN EVEN THE WORST DAYS INTO GOOD DAYS

Love is when he gives you a piece of your soul, that you never knew was missing.

TORQUATO TASSO

Love overcomes
hate. Love has no
colour. Love has
no orientation.

ADAM LAMBERT

No form of love
is wrong, so long
as it is love.

D. H. LAWRENCE

LOVE IS

beautiful.

BRENDON URIE

WE FOUGHT FOR OUR LOVE; IT SHOULD BE CELEBRATED

♥

Love does not
begin and end the
way we seem to
think it does.
Love is a battle,
love is a war;
love is growing up.

JAMES BALDWIN

BEING LOVED BY YOU GIVES ME THE COURAGE TO LIVE OPENLY

If you are not personally free to be yourself in that most important of all human activities – the expression of love – then life itself loses its meaning.

HARVEY MILK

The category is
love, ya'll, love.

BILLY PORTER

WE ALL DESERVE EQUAL RESPECT AND THE *right to love.*

STEFAN OLSDAL

I know by
experience
that the poets
are right:
love is eternal.

E. M. FORSTER

Now fill the
world with music,
love and pride.

LIN-MANUEL MIRANDA

Have you enjoyed this book? If so, find us on Facebook at **Summersdale Publishers**, on Twitter at **@Summersdale** and on Instagram at **@summersdalebooks** and get in touch. We'd love to hear from you!

www.summersdale.com